AF404440

James Hatari-Spielman

Do something! Now!

Ideas for the fight against climate change, poverty, hardship, hunger and capitalism

Publisher: Erich von Werner Verlag

Do something! Now!

Ideas for the fight against climate change, poverty, hardship, hunger and capitalism

ISBN: 978-3-948621-07-0

content

CHAPTER ONE

INTRODUCTION

"We say that what we all seek as the true meaning of life is, in my opinion, the experience of being alive, so that our life experience finds resonance on a purely physical level in our innermost being and reality, so that we can feel the enthusiasm of being alive.

These words of Joseph Campbell should remind us that life is what counts in the end. Humanity, empathy and justice belong to every life. These are basic values of being, which must be defended and for which it is worth risking everything.

This is also necessary because history teaches us that such a world has never existed before and will never exist without the great struggle. But many don't want to risk this fight anymore. They have given up and changes are, although they happen constantly, for them only a utopia and the talk of dreamers and do-gooders. What can the little man do? Aren't you just a grain of sand and so many? And anyway! Isn't the world much too complex to understand and change? Even if you did something. What good would it do?

That was always wrong. It's wrong and it will always be wrong. And we'll prove it to them!

Yet there is hope. It seems as if the age of awakening has come! More and more people are becoming critical and asking questions! They begin to realize that the pursuit of a better world is not the exclusive preserve of a godlike, superhero, or messiah who saves humanity from destruction. That it is not a matter of believing in a system that supposedly cares for the stupid sheep while selling them their own wool at the highest prices in the capitalist process. No, they feel that they are the heroes and that they can change the system.

Some will now call such words extremist, but they are not. They are courageous, just and true. Anyone who questions the existing economic, philosophical or social construct is an extremist to them and dangerous to those who have everything because they could lose it. So they're fighting those who fight for a better world. You're slandering her. They'll get dirty. Trying to twist their arguments and put the sheep to sleep. Bread and games. Consumption and entertainment. Sleep, dream and work.

And yet they can no longer control the world and it begins to waver and chaos. They have defamed the true fighters for freedom, democracy and justice for years and the result has been that the real extremists are now gaining more and more upper hand. In their struggle for their own egoism, they have opened the gates to those who wanted a totalitarian society. A grandiose failure like it couldn't have been worse.

What do we do now? Now it is time for the good and righteous to stand up and do for themselves what the system fails to do! Create a better world! This is democracy! This is activism, nothing will happen by itself. The chaos only gets bigger and bigger and who hopes that it overcomes itself, deceives itself.

"There is no natural law that brings withering to every power, nor are there any cycles, as some cultural pessimists may have recognized. Rather, it is probably simply human nature not to resist the downfall, but instead to stage the downfall as an inevitable celebration of the dead."

This is what Andreas Herteux writes and they are true words. Nothing changes on its own! The system was always questionable and now it's not strong enough. It needs committed people who change it and lead it back to the path of freedom, democracy and goodness or change it in such a way that it will be committed for all the future. And these people are us!

What have we done wrong?

Our media are flooded with bloody stories about war, climate change, hardship, hunger and death. But often we don't even notice them anymore. We'll displace them. That's human and yet so wrong.

Sometimes, when our awareness of these tragic realities reawakens, we quickly look for a way out, blame our political leaders and finally convince ourselves that there is nothing we can do about it. But that's a big lie! Everybody can do something! Helping others and giving something back has only been pushed into the background and has often disappeared behind the desire for a good consumer life. The fact that even at the lower level of the economic hierarchy people are treated with contempt and crushed is of no interest if they are not themselves affected. Injustice is everywhere. We just need to see. But when we see, the desire to act automatically awakens in every good heart.

Let us therefore no longer allow ourselves to be told the fairy tale of the grains of sand that are unconscious or even bribed. Let's look at reality! Let's act!

Breaking the cycle of doubt and restoring hope.

"The only thing necessary for the triumph of evil is that good people do nothing."

The words of Edmund Burke hit the nail on the head. If people manage to question supposed social norms, the world would already be a better place.

Efforts were needed by determined people to challenge the practice of slave trading, the separation of black and white, apartheid, etc. Evil was always "normal" and a change was unthinkable! Lies! Nothing but lies!

But people changed that! First a few, then many, and today the self-evident things of the past, such as slavery, are known for what they are: devilish and inhuman things to be ashamed of.

And yet not every person is someone who can use his life against racism or injustice. We can't demand that, and it never has been in history. There were always few and these few showed a perspective that many could follow. They turned an unsafe path into a somewhat safe one. It's true! It's true!

This book therefore does not require you to risk your life, but only to show you how you can make your contribution in small steps by collecting some small and one big idea with which you can make your world better. Some things you'll know, but you may never have done. Then see it as a reminder! You didn't have any ideas? Then we'll give you some! Join us! We are the pioneers of the great and the true! Come with us.

What's the matter with you? It is our world and our future! Let us create a great future full of freedom, justice and democracy! Give your life meaning. You can be a hero! In y-our way!

And so you also play your role in changing the world for the better. So you're a hero of light. It's your destiny!

CHAPTER TWO

The fight against climate change.

We don't want to go back too far: our climate is changing rapidly and at an enormous pace that gives cause for concern. Worried? What does that mean, worry? It's a climate disaster! But let us remain completely objective for the time being. Some of the striking differences observed in the last century are among others:

- Rising global sea level
- Changes in regional weather patterns that cause seasonal precipitation.
- Global average air and temperature rise

- In the long term, a far-reaching reduction in snow and ice cover was achieved.
- Changes in atmospheric and oceanic circulation

These changes are caused by additional heat in the climate system caused by the addition of greenhouse gases such as carbon dioxide, nitrous oxide or methane. The additional greenhouse gases are primary inputs from human activities such as the burning of fossil fuels (natural gas, coal, oil), deforestation, or progressive urbanization. These activities increase the amount of heat-storing greenhouse gases in the atmosphere. Or to put it simply: It's the fault of man!

Studies have shown that the changes observed to date in our climate are directly related to the increasing release of green-house gases into our environment. The argument that natural phenomena such as volcanic eruptions, the sun and other natural variability alone can effectively cause this rapid climate change, as some deniers would have sheep believe, is implausible. It is even dangerous nonsense, because the fact that there have always been changes in the climate has nothing to do with the fact that humans are now heavily involved. The glass may be half full, but if the person constantly adds water, it will overflow, no matter how much was already in it. This is not difficult to understand, but even with valid scientific information and data pointing to the plausibility of man-made climate change, there are still forces that do not accept or even deny the facts of climate change.

Don't you think they're hurting themselves? Of course, but the lure of short-term consumption or the temptation to gain power over people - through populist messages - are often stronger than the good and the true. The story is full of such behavior. It's the same old story. The greed and stupidity that has always harmed us, but which individuals or groups use temporarily.

We need to see through such mechanisms: It is rarely about content, but almost always about power, greed and income! Let us therefore reveal the true motives and show them to those who let themselves be seduced by false prophets!

In truth, most of the impacts of man-made climate change pose a risk to the sustainability of natural systems. These risks take the form of strong heat waves, disturbances in precipitation patterns, flooding or coastal flooding as a result of rising sea levels.

Once we have understood what climate change is, the question is what we can do about it. Our answer, of course, would be: renunciation and commitment, but of course we know that very few people can change from one day to the next.

Whoever demands this does not know man and that is one of the biggest mistakes of activism!

We also know that not everything that makes sense can be radically implemented because it would affect people's lives so negatively that the acceptance of the great struggle could be reduced. Here we differ massively from those radical forces that demand the total, while we stand solely for freedom, democracy and a better world.

In the end, we must also admit to ourselves that it is easy to be against something, but difficult to offer a better solution that takes all problems into account. Many committed activists have this problem and unfortunately ignore it. Something that shouldn't be happening to us!

But we look at the big picture! But first it should be about showing what everyone can do without being radical or extreme. The small steps that should sharpen and advance the consciousness of the masses.

That's why we recommend the small and simple things that really anyone can do. Let's march ahead!

- **Planting trees.**

  Planting trees is one of the easiest and most sustainable ways to positively influence our planet. Carbon dioxide (CO2) is a major greenhouse gas that literally "captures" the heat on our planet and above all leads to climate change. When trees grow, they absorb the available CO2 in the atmosphere. We must remove as much carbon as possible from the atmosphere to contain or prevent catastrophic events. We can decide to plant a tree ourselves or donate it to organizations that deal with tree planting. Trees produce oxygen that contributes to improving air quality and compensates for the harmful by-products of burning fossil fuels by storing carbon.

In addition, trees can significantly reduce air conditioning costs when planted strategically around a building. Because trees moderate the effect of the sun and thus provide a cooling effect. This leads to less Freon emissions, a dangerous odourless gas from air conditioning systems that has harmful effects on the ozone layer. Planting trees does not require a massive technological solution to reduce emissions. It is estimated that planting billions of trees worldwide could have significant impacts and potentials in reducing the impacts of climate change. So, roll up your sleeves and plant a tree today!

- **What foods to consume**

To mitigate climate change, the food we consume can play a role by either heating or reducing greenhouse gas emissions. So we can say that the food we eat can have a direct influence on our climate. So before you buy food or meat products from the shops, here are some factors you need to consider.

- How was it grown? ("Organic" or not)

- How much energy was used in the production process?
- How far did it travel to get to the shops?
- How low in the food chain is the product?

Livestock production and climate impact

The production of animal products requires a huge land area. Methane and nitrous oxide are two of the most important greenhouse gases. They are released during the production of farm animals.

The domestication of animals for food has proved to be totally counterproductive. To produce one kilogram of beef, at least seven kilograms of grain with other inputs such as water, energy, transport, etc. are needed.

The use of inorganic materials in agriculture

Chemicals such as pesticides and fertilizers are synthetically produced from fossil fuels. Synthetic nitrogen fertilizers produce nitrous oxide in soils, a greenhouse gas that is much stronger than carbon dioxide, causing more serious damage to our climate. Organic farms, on the other hand, depend on natural liquid manure and compost for the cultivation of their crops. Organic fertilisers have a good capacity to retain carbon and thus limit emissions into the atmosphere.

How are agricultural products transported?

Agricultural products that are produced locally are likely to require less distance, time and energy from the farms to our plates. The closer the production site moves, the lower the emissions that would have been recorded if fossil fuels had been burned. However, it should be noted that CO2 emissions from agricultural products depend primarily on the way in which they are produced and not on the distance between farms and our kitchens. So the next time you want to go shopping, make sure you buy food from organic and local sources.

<u>**Things you can do:**</u>

- **Reducing the consumption of meat and dairy products!**
- **Read labels and want to know what it says!**
- **Buy organic and local food if possible**
- **Grow your own food! That also works on the balcony in the city!**
- **Always keep yourself well informed!**
- **And of course, enlighten everyone you know!**

- **mobility**

Mobility is a key issue in the fight against climate change. Whether by land, sea or air. The shadow of horror is unfortunately almost always there. Let's take a little tour of the great mobility sinners:

aviation emissions

Records show that aviation accounts for more than 2% of global CO2 emissions. Air traffic emissions vary according to the duration of the flight, the number of passengers the aircraft carries, etc. For example, it is likely that an aircraft with fewer passengers will emit less CO2 because the carbon dioxide emissions of passengers will be reduced.

Flying is therefore a gigantic problem and it is not for nothing that the word "flying shame" has already become firmly established in the language and should definitely find further dissemination.

How you can reduce your CO2 emissions when flying:

- **Don't fly!**

- **Use other means of transport that are more environmentally friendly!**

- **Avoids less efficient airlines: Some airlines have**

modern aircraft that emit
less carbon and are better
able to fill seats.

- Take the direct flight: Airplanes need more fuel for take-off than for travel at high altitudes. For shorter flights, this accounts for the largest share of CO2 emissions.

- Take flights with more passengers: At peak times there are more passengers, which leads to lower emissions per person.

- And of course, enlighten everyone you know!

- **Cars**

  Cars give us a lot of mobility and freedom and also offer status and style for some sheep. Especially the latter confusion should not be underestimated. The car is not only functional, but also always emotional to look at. A crusade against the car is always also one against the feelings and thus possibly against the people themselves and that often prevents them from seeing what is good, just and right, because they feel attacked and defend the car because they want to defend themselves.

  However, this does not change the fact that motor vehicles have a considerable environmental impact on our climate. Our vehicles contribute significantly to the high CO2 emissions in the atmosphere. It takes a certain amount of energy to produce a car. Cars mostly run on fossil fuels, which cause serious environmental problems for our planet. From exploration to delivery, fossil fuels significantly distort the balance of our ecosystem. Cases of oil spills caused by fossil fuel exploration are a sad reminder of the costly damage done to our environment. In addition, our air quality is severely impaired by emissions from cars, trucks, etc. Car emissions not only affect our climate, they also pose a major health risk to people.

After years of struggle, we can now say that there is a general understanding of this problem.

The population sees these problems, but is often unable to react adequately to them for economic reasons.

Our aim must therefore be to further increase the pressure and sustainably promote the development of new technologies and ensure a cheaper dissemination, as well as extensive subsidization by the state.

As much as the fist may be clenched, we must also show understanding. Not for those who regard a car as an extension of their own ego, but for those whose existence would be endangered without the vehicle. A

balancing act that many honest activists would like to repress, but one
that is absolutely necessary.

What you can do:

- **Live a car-free life. That can be a
  little difficult because we have to
  move. But that would be a valuable way to reduce CO2 emissions into the atmosphere.**

- **Switch to electric cars: Electric
  cars were invented to reduce pol-
  lution and reduce carbon emissions into the climate.**

- **Use public transport: If more and
  more people park their cars and
  use the public transport system,**

we would have less CO2 emissions to worry about.

- **And of course, enlighten everyone you know!**

- **habitation**

Living is one of people's basic needs. However, according to the International Energy Agency (2015), housing accounts for 6% of global carbon dioxide emissions. Our households use LPG/gas oil for cooking, heating, cooling, etc., thus increasing CO2 emissions into the atmosphere. We are not even talking about compound effects, such as the CO2 balance in the production of objects or electricity.

In order to reduce the level of CO2 emissions from our homes, we can opt for new forms of homes that are very environmentally friendly.

Considering that concrete already contributes significantly to increased carbon emissions in the atmosphere, this makes rethinking all the more important. Environmentally friendly homes not only help combat climate change, but also reduce our energy and construction costs.

Types of environmentally friendly houses

Ground protected houses

These are houses that are built in laterally or underground. Only one side of the wall is visible, while the rest is covered with a heap of earth. Some of the advantages of this type of house are:

- o Minimal heating is required, saving energy costs.
- o They serve as very strong storm protection, since part or all of the house is underground. This is very important considering the further consequences of climate change.

<u>prefabricated houses</u>

These houses are being built outside the property. They are brought to the site and assembled there, which saves a lot of personnel and construction costs. The advantages of this series of houses are:

- o They are made of environmentally friendly materials.
- o The windows and headlights are fixed. These help to save heat and thus reduce energy costs.
- o They're built to withstand natural disasters.

<u>So-called earth ships</u>

These forms of houses are built from natural and upward facing materials. They are designed to be self-running and sufficient. This means that they are less dependent on public utilities and function mainly with built-in re-sources. The advantages of these houses are:

- o Thermal solar heating and cooling that keeps you fresh in summer and warm in winter.
- o Solar and wind power
- o Independent waste wa-ter treatment.

<u>shipping container houses</u>

These are houses of reused shipping containers. They are becoming more and more popular because of their immense advantages, which also include:

- Less concrete and cement consumption, which helps reduce carbon emissions.
- Much cheaper than bricks and steel
- They help to withstand extreme weather conditions.

Of course, we activists also know that most of the houses are already standing or that many people have no choice but to take the accommodation that is offered because the lack of rented accommodation can be a problem everywhere. Then the fight begins again in the small!

<u>**What you can do:**</u>

- o **Always live climate compliant!**

- o **Convert your existing house in an environmentally friendly way! Get that oil heater out of here! Dams right and use energy saving lamps and energy saving devices!**

- Live consciously at all times! Do without the heating if it is not really cold! Lights and equipment should be switched off when not in use! The list of possibilities is almost endless!

- Always use an ecological energy supply!

- And, of course, to enlighten everyone you know!

CHAPTER THREE

Combating poverty and hardship

Poverty can be described as a condition in which a person or community lacks the conditions for a minimum standard of living. Poor people are not only unable to access economic resources for their needs, but also, more importantly, have no way to live in dignity.

This means that income levels are so low that basic everyday needs cannot be met. People living in poverty may have no or only limited access to health care, education, housing, food, etc. The poverty rate varies from country to country, but it is a global phenomenon, although in some countries it is mitigated by the social system. Whether the social systems really help or only suppress or delay a revolution or an uprising is controversial.

Global poverty

The poverty rate in Western countries has been drastically reduced since the era of the industrial revolution. Progress in agriculture has improved yields and food availability. Medicine made just as much progress as the workers' movement, which for the first time was able to assert real rights for all. Most important factor for this were technical innovations that improve life for many people. However, not all regions benefited from this development.

For example, sub-Saharan Africa is still struggling with the challenges of poverty, as half the world's poor live there. World Bank figures indicate that people live in extreme poverty on $1.90 a day, if you want to call it living. A reality that many people should turn a blind eye to and reflect upon. But what does poverty, whether in an industrialised country or in Africa, really mean for those affected?

Impact of poverty

Poverty characterizes life and has been proven in completely different areas:

- **Education:**
  Studies show that children from

impoverished families have less access to adequate education. Other poverty-related factors such as health care, the social environment or violence can also limit the success of a child in terms of education. Children need attention, unconditional love and a stable environment to learn effectively. Poverty does not allow these conditions to flourish, which limits the children's ability to learn. Those who have no access to education, however, lack a basic means of advancement.

- **Social exclusion**

People are social animals. Our daily interactions open up new horizons

and create a number of untapped opportunities. People living in poverty
are limited to their own space. They
are cut off from the mainstream of
social participation and inclusion. Be
it for financial reasons, shame or by
giving yourself up.

* **hunger**

One of the dehumanizing aspects of
poverty is hunger. People who earn a
meager income find it extremely difficult to feed and are therefore physi-
cally and mentally in eternal helpless-
ness. Malnutrition is another aspect
of the hunger of people living in
poverty. For some, nutrition is just a
need to suppress appetite, and so

their meals are nutrient-free to support the development and maintenance of the body. A vicious circle that is often unstoppable.

- **lodgings**

Poverty can be linked to homelessness and miserable living conditions. The inhabitants of large urban slums around the world live in poverty. For many poor people in industrialized countries, only poor residential areas remain. Homelessness has forced many children to live in state care even though they have parents.

- **violence**

Poverty produces violence, and violence produces more violence. Children from economically disadvantaged families are vulnerable to misdemeanours and crimes. Many children and young people in poor homes are likely to participate in crime as a necessary tool for survival. Can you blame them for that?

- **Social Vices**

In addition to violence, other social vices such as drug abuse, prostitution, etc. can be seen as linked to poverty.

- **Infrastructure**

  Access to electricity, water, sanitation and infrastructure is lacking in poor communities or districts. Some developing countries have water supply networks in their cities. This means that people can get clean and purified water from the taps in their homes. Unfortunately, many poor communities do not have access to this distribution network, so they have to buy drinking water from suppliers. Others go long distances to get access to drinking water from rivers and streams or the only tap water in the community.

  Electricity is another key to a comfortable life. Many low-income families have no access to electricity, so they can use bush lamps and candles as light sources in their homes.

Causes of poverty

Causes of poverty can sometimes be subjective, but it is generally associated with social problems, such as

- illiteracy
- overpopulation
- unemployment
- government failure
- Mental performance and limitations of the individual
- Climate change.
- Unjust economic system
- exploitation

Ideas for poverty reduction

The fight against poverty has become a global challenge, not only for governments and non-governmental organisations, but also for us, those who want a world of equality and opportunities for all. No man may be deprived of the dignity of life. Vital necessities such as water, food and medicines should be the least of people's worries. Here, too, we must not wait for a few superheroes or even trust the governments, but take action ourselves. At least on a small scale:

- **donate money**

  Donating money is an effective way that we can use to fight the scourge of poverty in our world. Studies show that every fifth person lives in extreme poverty. They live in slums, without adequate shelter and care. Donating money to them can help break the cycle of poverty and give them the appearance of a decent life. Your donation can help create a better future and further reduce the inequality of the world.

Many people rightly feel great despair and sadness about the extent of poverty in the world. They wrongly believe that it is far beyond our ability to bring about change, given the large number of people living in poverty. In fact, they too must acknowledge that donating to the poor through charitable organizations is an effective way to fight poverty. There are many charities and NGOs dedicated to reaching low-income families in need around the world. Over the years, they have taken on the responsibility of coordinating people's donations to reach the disadvantaged regardless of location. While some people doubt the effectiveness and reach of charitable donations, statistics show that the number of extremely poor in the world is decreasing. The reports show that the number of extremely poor people has fallen by an average of 50 million per year since 1999. Your little donations can be anything it takes to make a difference. Only the money has to arrive.

There are millions of nonprofit organizations around the world asking for funds from donors. Stories about mis-management and fraud are widespread. They are despicable, as are the protagonists of evil, who pay homage to self-interest and cheat the poorest of the poor on their daily bread.

Therefore, it is important that we create a checklist for the organization we want to donate to. It is important that we ensure that we choose a charity that fits our philanthropic beliefs.

We must not donate our money for its own sake! Don't donate and then look the other way. That would be hypocrisy and buying a good conscience! No, we have to guarantee that everything gets where it needs to go!

And basically, we don't donate either. Instead, we must see our donations as investments that actually help the poor. A completely different and much better way of thinking: We do not subsidize poor people, but invest in the future of our planet! It is therefore important that every cent is used sensibly.

Here are a few things to keep in mind before choosing the charity we donate to:

- **How legitimate are they?**
- **How well do you know this organization?**

- **Are my donations tax de-
  ductible?**
- **Make sure that you can view
  the charity's report and eva-
  luations.**

Therefore always make sure that your donation arrives where it is needed. Always!

- **Social commitment:**

Countless people live in a bubble of stability and comfort. But they the poverty and neglect around them. At least as long as they're not sheep. But the seeing people are stimulated, encouraged and animated by reality to do something against the prevailing conditions and to change the situation. Poverty is a social problem, and everyone must contribute to its significant reduction. One of the first steps towards poverty reduction is understanding what it is. Membership in poverty reduction social groups offers volunteers the opportunity to learn how poverty mechanisms work, how they affect families, and how people can get out of poverty and achieve a more sustainable lifestyle. Be an ambassador for the poorest! Become their hero!

- **Voluntary work to fight poverty**

Voluntary work in the fight against poverty requires a lot of time and energy. The good thing is you're

doing it for something you passio-
nately believe in. Go to your table and
help! Collect expired food and donate
it! The ways are unlimited!

- **Organization of fundraising events**

  Fundraisers are a great thing. Organ-
  sieire itself to raise funds for the poor.
  You can join local fundraising groups
  or start one yourself. Just start today.

- **Consume consciously!**

  Remember that many products are
  made in the most miserable of

circumstances and their low price may drive other products off the market that would allow poor people a better life. Therefore, act consciously and inform yourself exactly about your consumption.

CHAPTER FOUR

Become an activist, demonstrate and be political!

Activism consists of efforts to promote social, political, economic and environmental reforms in society, to intervene in processes or to participate directly in them. Activism is acting for one thing.

This cause goes beyond utterance; it is the relentless attitude and belief in the change of order. Activism can be routine or conventional, e.g. door-to-door switching, meetings, rallies, street protests, etc. It can also be unconventional or dependent on the strategies of the initiators. Anything goes if you want!

Activism has contributed to calling into question previous social norms such as racism, slavery, inequality, women's rights, etc.

Actionism is therefore a good thing, although individuals or groups want to abuse the commitment of people for their own totalitarian purposes, under false flags. These black sheep need to be identified and uncovered.

A true activist is someone who questions the politics of evil in order to achieve a good or better goal. An active main goal is not to gain power, but to show commitment in defending what seems right. The good is an eternal ideal and it must be defended. Those who stand up for it and a better world can therefore never act wrongly.

In the past, activism was mainly spread through literature, brochures, books, etc., in order to get the public to work for the justice of their cause. Today, activists use modern media tools such as social media to improve civic engagement and rallies. The new era has created a multitude of possibilities that would have been dreamed of in the past. Let's use them all!

Become an Activist

Activists are committed to social change. Most of the time we don't know what power we have until we decide to exercise it. This is something you don't expect from stunned sheep, and the powerful are often hit unexpectedly and with relentless harshness.

Activism can therefore be loud. Always. He may also be violent. But his goal must always be freedom, equality, democracy and a better world. The end does not always justify the means and violence is to be rejected as an active form of violence.

When are you an activist? When you begin to take responsibility and have developed an awareness of the good!

Activism does not require specific skills or a specific professional background. All you need to be an activist is passion, determination and knowledge. What you can do:

- **Find your topic!**

    There are many social and political problems that we face today. Pick out some and then look for ways to denounce them and solve them!

o **Try to gain knowledge!**

You have the better arguments! You just have to know them and be able to bring them across! Never forget that!

Don't ever let a lack of knowledge play you down!

o **Invest your time**

Time is an important commodity. What could be better than using her for a big cause? What feeling can be greater than to become a fighter of light?

- **Always lead by example**

  As activists, we must practice what we preach in order to advance our cause. There are already enough hypocrites and careerists. The movement of the future must be pure!

- **Joining an NGO ("Non governmental organization")**

  Joining an NGO is much better than sitting at home waiting for something to change. Our ideal world can only become reality if we strive to change it. NGOs help to bring about social and positive changes in our society.

o **Demonstrate and be political**

Showing interest in politics is very important for an activist. Most of the social and political issues that affect us today are decided by politicians. For example, if you believe in the rights of homosexuals, you should be able to identify candidates who have spoken out for homosexual rights in campaigns and interviews. Equipped with this knowledge, you can decide which candidates receive your votes. Basically, there is nothing that is not political in any way! Never forget that and always be mindful!

The indifference of the voters and the lack of protests against the evils of society have fuelled the complacency

and mismanagement of our politicians. The sheep have refused to hold
their decision-makers accountable,
but their actions and inaction affect us
all. So don't be a sheep! Don't let y-
ourself get carried away and shear,
but know what they're doing and why
they're doing it. Do what, then? It's
simple:

- **Vote for politicians who are guided by our cause**

- **But don't make any wrong compromises.**

  Never choose the lesser evil, but only the one you can believe in. If there isn't one, then the system has failed, and not you.

- **But never lose your faith in democracy, though.**

There is no better form of government. Don't let totalitarian hypocrites fascinate you. Pied Pipers who want to establish a dictatorship with the mask of philanthropy! Expose them and if they don't, fight them again and again!

- **Never forget: Politics concerns us all**

  Decisions or laws made by politicians influence us in one way or another.

- **You have the right to be dissatisfied!**

  Don't let them tell you there's always a compromise. Sometimes there isn't.

- **Democracy does not only take place on election day!**

  Don't let them talk you into thinking democracy ends on election night. Democracy does not only take place in parliaments. Your actionism is lived democracy. You're on the right side, and whoever denies it is on the wrong side.

- **Stand up for what you believe:**

We all have different opinions and views on certain topics. An active interest in politics would put us in a better informed position and help us find ways to change the status quo. It needs you and your commitment.

- **Participation in demonstrations and protests**

  Demonstrations and protests are a means of democracy. A demonstration is a mass action against or for a particular cause. Demonstrations can be peaceful and in some cases violent. Demonstrations are generally regarded as successful if they showed a high level of participation.

  If we find that there is a lack of social justice on an issue, or if we take a different stand on a legislative issue, etc., we should meet people with similar views on the issue and develop strategies for protest or civil demonstrations.

Or less abstract: Go demonstrate and show them that you will never accept a bad world!

What you should know before taking part in a demonstration:

- Do you know the local laws about protests and demonstrations? Avoid violating these laws! Sometimes it happened faster than you'd think! Therefore inform yourself exactly and above all know your rights!

- Make your messages visually clear e.g. by banners or posters! Remember that you may be photographed or filmed and then your message is practically immortalized! The effect is much greater than with a purely verbal message!

- Prepare yourself by taking enough water, recharging your cell phones, and so on.

- Go with a friend or meet friends there! You can break a finger, but five fingers is a fist!

- Encourage your environment to accompany you! Convince it of your cause!

- Wear comfortable things!

- Do not use water for attacks. Pepper spray or tear gas; it just gets worse. Use milk, lemon juice etc.

- Know the demonstration area and know where to retreat if necessary!

- Share your experiences and create a circle of activists in your environment!

- Come to the demonstration in an environmentally friendly way and act according to your convictions!

CHAPTER FIVE

Fight against capitalism

Capitalism can be defined as a system in which private individuals or companies own capital goods. The production of products and services is based on supply and demand, i.e. on a general market. The opposite is a system in which production is planned, controlled and owned by the general public.

An economy is capitalist if private individuals or companies predominantly operate the production factors. These are labour, land and capital. Recent publications speak of a new factor of production, behavior, and thus of Behavioral Capitalism, another variety of capitalism that has developed through the beautiful new Internet world.

The owners of these production factors exercise control over the companies and thus indirectly also over society, although they are also subject to market forces. The state still has the possibility to intervene, but apparently often fails. The effects of capitalism are mitigated in some countries by a social system.

Don't fall into the socialism trap!

The fundamental question of whether capitalism is bad is a difficult one. Skilful capitalists always point to the failure of socialist systems and many activists are unfortunately foolish enough to present failed communist ideas as a serious alternative and thus logically meet with rejection from the majority of the population.

A smart activist doesn't fall into the socialism trap. The counterpart to capitalism is not socialism! This has to be hammered into every activist! Socialism failed and led exclusively to totalitarian dictatorships, in which people were demonstrably much worse off than in evil capitalism! This does not mean, however, that capitalism has no alternative. We must overcome it in its present form, without coming from the frying pan into the fire. For this, however, we need new concepts, such as that of Alternative Hegemony (AH Model), which is presented in the last chapter. A true fighter for a better world therefore distanced himself from all the Maos, Stalins, Lenins & Co and despised these monsters as much as the greedy big capitalists.

Why capitalism is flawed

"The profit motive. If it is the primary goal of an economic system, it promotes unhealthy competition that inspires people to be selfish. People tend to care more about their livelihoods than their lives."

Martin Luther King

- **Inequality**:
  Capitalism promotes a system in which wealth is not evenly distributed, leading to imbalances. The capitalist uses his capital and assets to

acquire more assets. In addition, the capitalist passes on assets and wealth to his children and leaves the disadvantaged group without anything behind.

- **Formation of monopolies and oligopolies**

Capitalism creates market power and limited access to production factors. A capitalist can maximize his profits by, for example, paying less wages. This explains why companies' profit margins continue to rise without workers' wages rising accordingly.

- **It promotes greed.**

  For capitalism, it's all about profits. The social welfare of employees takes second place.

- **Capitalism and poverty**

  Poverty is one of the key challenges we face today. Millions of people are denied the right to live a life worth living. There is a great divide between the poor and the rich, for wealth is in the hands of a few.

  There are activists who say, "Capitalism should ensure that the rich and powerful assert their position by enslaving the majority world under bad working structures with little or no rights."

The solution

It is of course possible to take numerous individual measures against capitalism, but we do not want to fight symptoms, we want to fight the cause, i.e. the errors of capitalism.

For a long time, this seemed impossible. Alternative systems have failed cracking or, like socialism, turned out to be much worse than capitalism ever was, and yet there are now ideas that should be known as any activist interested in capitalism. The largest and most realistic of these will be briefly presented in the last chapter: The model of Alternative Hegemony (AH Model).

CHAPTER SECHS

The Model of Alternative Hegemony (AH Model)- A Way to a Better World

The AH Model aims to offer solutions for which we are not prepared. The search for a better future requires a comprehensive approach, but also honesty. Part of this honesty is that we already have a world and cannot start from scratch. We must therefore make something new and better out of what is there, and we must not dream that we can start all over again. We activists must take people with us and not try to force a future on them. Such an attempt would end in a dictatorship that a true activist who stands up for the good could only detest. So don't become what you hate!

It is undisputed that the time for a major change is more favourable than ever. It's not chaos or complex, it's just the time to finally lead the world into a better future! If not now, when?

Yes, as Andreas Herteux aptly analyses, we are faced with a change of times characterized by 5 factors that are in constant interaction:

- The future handling of new technologies (e.g. digitisation, biotechnology, human optimisation).
- The rise of new competitors on the world markets. (e.g. Asian countries)

- The weakness of the Western world has led to instability, weakened confidence in existing orders, impaired competitiveness and promoted China's political ascent.

- environmental change (e.g. through climate change, resource exploitation, environmental degradation)

- Overpopulation and lack of life, please. (due to the demographic development of the African continent).

Every real activist must know these 5 points and also that they cannot be separated from each other! No one demands that you become active in all of them, but you need to know the connections!

The change of times comes along anyway and it is up to us to shape it in such a way that in the end there is a better world and not a worse one! That's your responsibility, new activist!

But how can the AH Model help?

The Model of Alternative Hegemony (AH Model)

"The Model of Alternative Hegemony is an evolution and a corrective of the capitalist system. The goal is global peace, freedom and global prosperity.

It transforms capitalism into a value capitalism, democratizes the key industries of the future and acts according to market laws.

It does not exert any compulsion, but diverts the desire for profit or benefit maximization of enterprises and states in such a way that this maximization is possible only if these serve the well-being of all."

The Alternative Hegemony Model (AH Model)

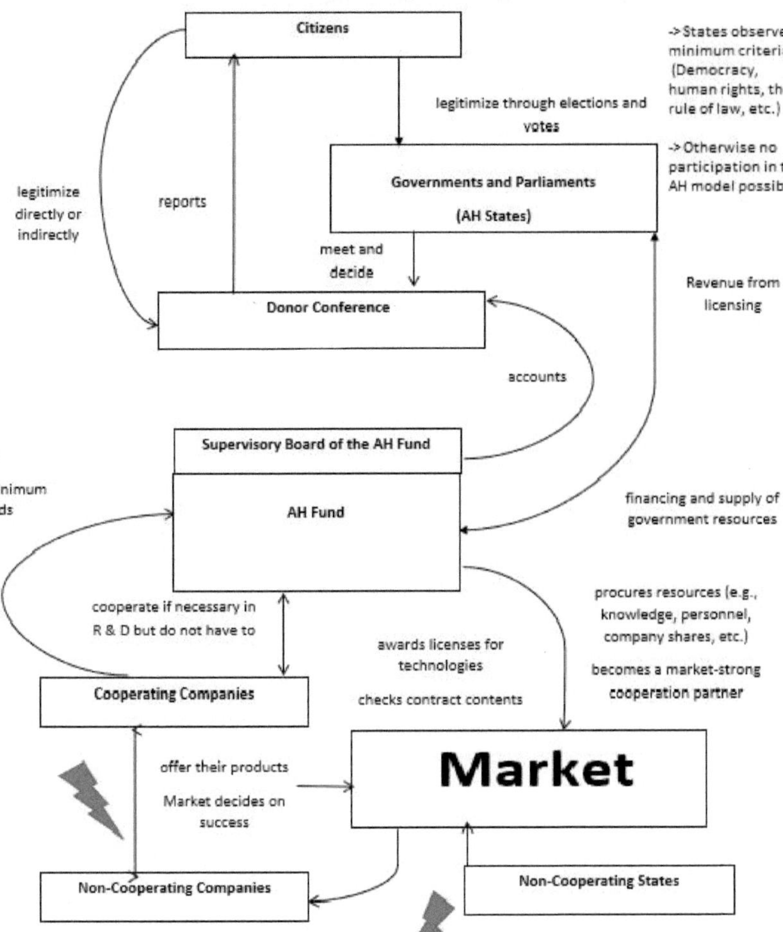

essure from the market or the desire for profit
aximization makes it attractive to become an AH
mpany

➔ creating better conditions for workers

➔ In the market, the one who adheres to these minimum standards prevails

imited access to specific technologies or products

Market pressure makes desire for participation in the AH Fund attractive

➔ Compliance with minimum standards is mandatory

➔ Improvement of the life of the citizens

➔ Abolition of authoritarian system

It is an evolution of the previous international political and economic system. It develops this further, retains existing structures and diverts negative dynamics. There is therefore no need to stop the tide, because man cannot do that, but he can use it to his advantage, in which the AH Model educates states as well as companies to behave in a valuable way, from which everyone benefits in the end. [...] In the model of alternative hegemony, however, coercion does not exist, but only voluntariness. [...] They will continue to act selfishly, but the model of alternative hegemony will create a new production factor that will be central to profit maximization or maximum benefit: Values.

This factor of production and success changes the conditions of economic activity and with it the system itself, without having to give up even a spark of selfishness, for the AH system makes use of the same forces that prevail in the previous capitalist system, but guides them in a new direction: the invisible hand of the market becomes the invisible hand of education. And capitalism is educated, not man. The cold market economy becomes value capitalism and this could become a blessing for the world in the long run.

Sounds good? Or utopian? How is this to be realized?

Well, this succeeds by occupying a central field: research and development of new technologies. They are bundled within the framework of the AH Model. This is done through an AH Fund, which is financed by the states participating in the AH model with 2% of their respective GDP.

The AH Fund develops new and improves old technologies and subsequently offers licenses and patents. With his capital, he creates his own research facilities, acquires companies, cooperates with others and tries, in a simplified way, to gain maximum market power in a short period of time. The aim is to be the technological or developing market leader in all key industries of the future at the research level. Science would thus be democratized and would no longer lie in the hands of capitalist corporations or authoritarian states, but in the hands of the people themselves.

Participation in the AH Fund is in turn linked to compliance with a set of values. These criteria (e.g. human rights, freedom of the press, social standards, etc.) are constantly monitored. Countries that refuse to meet the criteria are excluded from the AH Fund and thus ultimately excluded from technological progress in the medium to long term, but in-directly encouraged by the invisible hand of education for voluntary adaptation. Non-compliant states will tend to adhere to fun-damental values in the future or to develop towards them with the help of the complying states. Not out of goodness or insight, but out of calculation and egoism, in order to participate in technical progress. Values thus become a success factor at the state level.

This of course requires corresponding power, and in the AH system this is not generated by socialist experiments, but by the market itself, because the AH fund is part of it and the price for its products, in this case patents and licences, are money and the observance of values. Value capitalism thus emerges from the system and the ugly, insatiable caterpillar can thus become a beautiful butterfly, because the AH Fund becomes a dominant market participant through its capital, which can act offensively solely through the aforementioned capital, as far as the procurement of resources, which also includes participation in companies, is concerned. Of course, this should not create an opaque juggernaut; we have enough of them ready, but a transparent and democratic structure.

The AH Fund is managed by a Board of Directors analogous to a stock corporation. It is controlled by a committee ("Supervisory Board") composed of democratically legitimised members from individual countries. It is also subject to intensive transparency obligations vis-à-vis the public.

The AH Model therefore combines and democratises scientific competence, conducts basic research, develops technologies and makes them available to the markets of the countries participating in the AH model. The production and distribution are carried out by cooperating companies which continue to operate according to market economy principles.

The AH Fund therefore grants licenses for use and production to cooperating companies that meet the criteria in return for payment. It not only bears itself at some point, but also generates profits which flow back into the Member States and can solve urgent problems there. But we're not there yet. Let's stay with the licensees.

These companies operate normally on the market and are subject to competition. By resorting to modern technologies and licenses, however, they have a competitive advantage over value deniers because they can use the research of the AH system as the basis for their individual products. Here again the same principle applies as for states: they will continue to behave selfishly and want to achieve maximum benefit for themselves. There is no doubt about that, and they should. But there is now a central difference:

Now the success factors have changed, because the easiest way to maximise profit is to adhere to values (e.g. working conditions, wages, co-determination). If these are disregarded, cooperation with the AH Fund is not possible. Values thus become a production factor such as labour, land, capital and behaviour. Companies will therefore adapt voluntarily. Not out of kindness, but out of calculation. Market forces are thus steered in a positive direction. The invisible hand of education works again, without any compulsion and without any regimentation.

An old dream comes true: capitalism is corrected in its outgrowths and the revealed butterfly shines in its most beautiful colours. Value capitalism or the value market economy is emerging, is spreading at least in *the West, can confront guided capitalism, outstrip it and subsequently be successful worldwide.*

What's it going to cost people? Nothing, because it doesn't take anything away, it gives. The AH system does not touch culture or identity, has no coercion, does not demand the abolition of nations, or takes away opportunities for democratic co-determination - unless it is   a brutal and inhuman dictatorship. In this case, the AH Model will try to change them in favour of freedom. The same applies to companies. The model of alternative hegemony does not interfere with their freedom, but merely offers massive competitive advantages.

The fact that nation states, government systems, identities or cultural peculiarities are preserved means that the population as a whole can be expected to be generally accepted, since the population ultimately benefits from the commitment to values by states and companies on the one hand and from the reflux of income from the AH Fund into the member states on the other. These can be used there for urgent challenges, such as the pension system.

The AH Model therefore not only restrains capitalism, it also generates wealth and enforces values without coercion, through the forces of the market. Greed creates good with it. Country by country and company by company will thus be transformed into an alternative hegemony. Not out of conviction, but out of self-interest, but must we be interested in that? Man will be freer than ever before, because not only will the milieu struggles be contained, but also behavioural capitalism can be regulated for the first time with appropriate legislation to protect people. The age of collective individualism thus becomes one of freedom and not of invisible fetters.

So this is the basic idea of the model of alternative hegemony. In the best case we therefore have a flourishing and better earth, in which prosperity, freedom and peace reign.

In the worst case, the AH system creates a counterweight to the future power of authoritarian systems, which is equal to it. We need these anyway for the struggle for existence. It may take many decades, but it is a new world community that takes cultural peculiarities into account and is neverthel-ess forward-looking. An alternative hege-mony that educates for good."

The last pages and the illustration were provided to us by the Erich von Werner Gesellschaft and Mr. Andreas Herteux, the developer of the model, for a unique reprint.

Why the AH Model should inspire us!

The model of alternative hegemony inspires us because it brings a real perspective. So far, the answer to capitalism has always been socialism. But as hard as it is for us, it failed mercilessly and for many people, on whose support we depend, it is a red cloth.

We make it easy for the enemies of the good to discredit us if our answer to problems of the system is only the creation of an even bigger problem.

For many activists this is difficult to accept, but do we want to live as we once did in the GDR or the Soviet Union? No, no one seriously wants that!

Do we attach great importance to living in countries like China or North Korea right now? Then even the smallest activism would be life-threatening!

So far, however, there has hardly been a namable alternative to capitalism, now there is: The model of alternative hegemony (AH model), which transforms capitalism into a value market economy.

Why not use capitalism and its greed for a better world just as it has used millions of people for its purposes?

Why not turn the system around?

It's the smarter way! It is the path of actionism in the 21st century!

Therefore, we should learn to understand the Model of Alternative Hegemony and then disseminate it.

Its implementation is not a utopia, but possible! Let's fight for it by spreading it and claiming it! For our good and for the good of all mankind!

CHAPTER SEVEN

The path of change

This brings us to the end of our little booklet, which hopefully provided an important overview without overburdening us with facts. For the purely factual questions there is much more detailed literature and you will surely find it.

Yes, there would be so much more to say, but we don't have to, because we just wanted to wake you up or, when you woke up, motivate you to move on!

Farther than ever before in the struggle for freedom, democracy, justice, love and truthfulness. In the struggle for a better world for all people.

We need you, and now it's your turn. You know what you need to know. There are no more excuses now! Go ahead. Get active! Do it! Now.

About the publishing house

Erich von Werner Verlag

Birkenfelder road 3

97842 Karbach

Homepage:

https://www.erichvonwernerverlag.de/

Email:

Info@erichvonwernerverlag.de

Facebook:

https://de-de.facebook.com/erichvonwernerver-
lag

About the author

James Hatari-Spielman

James "Jim" Harari-Spielman (born 1989) is a US-American activist and author who works for a better world. Jim Harari-Spielman comes from New York, but is active worldwide.
He always remains controversial and stimulating.